NOT ALL MUD AND SCRUMS

RUGBY UNION BEFORE PROFESSIONALISM

T0334807

NOT ALL MUD AND SCRUMS

RUGBY UNION BEFORE PROFESSIONALISM

GORDON ALLAN

THE
Alpha
PRESS

The right of Gordon Allan to be identified as author of this work
has been asserted in accordance with the Copyright,
Designs and Patents Act 1988.

Published by

The Alpha Press
18 Chichester Place
Brighton BN2 1FF

First published 1996

ISBN 1 898595 19 4

Printed and bound by Biddles Ltd, King's Lynn and Guildford

Preface and Acknowledgements

This little book, which is just the right length for a train journey, perhaps to an international match, is not topical. It was never intended to be, having largely been written before professionalism turned the rugby union game inside out. Nor is it controversial: I do not like the word, let alone what it connotes. I wrote it for my own pleasure, in kaleidoscopic style, to distil recollections of nearly half a century spent following rugby in one way or another. I hope it will give modest pleasure to those readers who, like me, were introduced to the game in simpler times and who still take a simple view of it, in spite of everything.

I wish to thank *The Times* newspaper for permission to reproduce excerpts from material previously published, and also extend my thanks to Allsport/Hulton Deutsch, Sport & General, the Press Association, and the Scottish Rugby Union for permission to reproduce the photos, which are also individually acknowledged.

"The history of the game actually consists of a few facts and a large body of legends."

Chris Laidlaw, *Mud In Your Eye*
(Pelham Books, 1973)

My father was at the opening of Murrayfield in 1925 and saw Scotland beat England to win their first grand slam. It was, he used to tell me, the most exciting match he had ever seen. He himself never played much rugby, preferring soccer, but in his opinion rugby was the better game to watch; the highlight of his active career was playing in an army game with Jack Warren, who had been a Scotland three-quarter just before the First World War. I think it may have been on the momentous 1925 occasion that his companion, a woman who knew enough about soccer but nothing at all about rugby, turned to him, after somebody had kicked a goal, and in her innocence said, "Hard luck – just over."

A little more than twenty years later, my own latent interest in rugby was unexpectedly kindled. I was then entering my 'teens at the Aberdeen Grammar School, having up to that time done my utmost to avoid all forms of organized sport; often I played truant from midweek games afternoons at Rubislaw and sneaked off to a cowboy film. But Dallas – "Dally" – Allardice, a games master at the Grammar and a member of the highly successful Former Pupils team, was playing scrum half for Scotland during this period (the school was given a day off when he was awarded his first cap), and my father suggested that I ought to show my respect for "Dally's" example by participating in at least one of the school's sporting activities, if only out of loyalty.

Thus did I start playing. Thus am I now entitled to answer the usual question with "Yes, I've played a bit." I was hopeless, but contrived to enjoy myself in the lower reaches, the fifth, sixth, seventh and eighth teams, referred, oddly enough, by the long-suffering "Dally", who might have been thought just the man to have charge of the first fifteen, but for some reason wasn't. I can remember being shown by him how to bind with the hooker, but I did not endure as a prop and was moved back to the second row, which I soon decided is the natural home of all incompetent players, since mistakes made in the thick of the scrum are more easily disguised there than anywhere else on the field. If I had ever needed a pen-name as a rugby writer, I would have chosen "Second Row".

"Dally" had served in the Commandos in the war, and when he returned to the Grammar he became the pivot, brilliant and unpredictable, of probably the best team ever to represent the Former Pupils. They were led by Dr Johnny Innes, a centre who captained Scotland after the war, having been first capped before it, and on one wing there was Doug Smith, also a doctor, who was destined to be the manager of the British Lions in New Zealand in 1971, startling all concerned by correctly forecasting the result of the test series.

A year or so after the unofficial Scottish clubs championship had been won by Innes's FPs, there was an equally fine school side, big, fast and skilful, who went undefeated through a season of fourteen matches. Ernie Michie was in it, a lock forward who played for Scotland and toured South Africa with the 1955 Lions; I have seen a photograph of him, in his kilt, piping the Lions on to the field at Durban. Ron Comber, another member of that school pack, was a wing forward (the word flanker had not then been coined) who, with the direct-hit approach that earned him the nickname "Bomber", eventually metamorphosed into a three-quarter, and once, I think, scored two tries in a Murrayfield trial.

As for me, when I returned from National Service in Germany, where I had played a little soccer and snooker and umpired a little cricket, I played no more than three seasons, intermittently, for the FPs' third or fourth teams. I never trained – I did not want to, and it would have been difficult anyway, as I was working night shift on the local newspaper by then. I just received my card and turned up, at Rubislaw, Seafield, Hazlehead, or the point of departure for the coach to Lossiemouth, Dundee, Arbroath, or wherever. Naturally they put me in the second row, but I can recall at least one outing at wing forward, with instructions, solemnly given to me in the coach, to mark the blind side: and I was no tearaway.

Retiring to the touchline, I watched the FPs season after season; and I still follow them from afar. They have had their highs and their lows but never a concentration of talents to match that of the late nineteen-forties. Towards the end of his playing career, with FPs by that time no more than an average side, "Dally", though he had lost speed, would often be selected at wing forward or stand-off half. Even in his prime he was criticized for being too individualistic, for losing touch with the support, and he did tend to think and move too quickly for the rest of his team. But as he also tended to think and move too quickly for the opposition, and scores accrued, this was not the weakness it could have been.

"Dally" was an all-round sportsman, like another Aberdonian and Scotland scrum half of a later vintage, Ian McCrae, from the Gordonians club, fierce rivals of the Grammar FPs. McCrae had played as an inside forward in Aberdeen junior football and on one occasion a professional club approached him, doing all they could to meet his wishes concerning salary, accommodation and training. Finally McCrae said: "There's just one more thing. I'll require every Saturday afternoon off to play rugby."

In the summer of 1960 I left for Fleet Street and, apart from eighteen months with *The Scotsman* in Edinburgh and nine months on a north London weekly, I have been there ever since. In March 1965, within a month of joining *The Times* as a sports sub-editor, I was reporting on the first of my hundreds of rugby matches – London Scottish against Moseley at the Richmond Athletic Ground, a place that has come to feel like a second home to me. *Times* correspondents in those days were not named, and I was A Staff Reporter – and proud of it – until the paper's policy in this, as in much else, changed two years later. It is one of my little boasts now, relating me as it does to a remote past, that I have worked for *The Times* when its offices were still in Queen Victoria Street at Blackfriars, when it still carried small advertisements on the front page, and when anonymity was still the rule for its writing journalists.

Also in March 1965, I made my first appearance in the press box at Twickenham, not as a reporter but as a guest of *The Times* rugby correspondent, U. A. Titley; the U stood for Uel, deriving from his father's name, Samuel. Uel insisted that only his initials should be used, and he was hurt when "Uel" accidentally got into print. I sat between him and Harold Day, and the old Leicester and England wing, who was writing for the *Observer*, I think, and who asked whether I had ever played rugby. In an ideal world, "Yes – Scotland, Barbarians and British Lions" would have been my answer, but a mumbled and modest affirmative was all I could give. The Queen, a tiny figure in pale blue, was in the stand opposite, and as she took her seat Titley leaned across to Day, saying in an awestruck voice, "It's the Monarch, Harold, the Monarch." The match – England against Scotland – is remembered solely for its last minute, when Andy Hancock, the Northampton wing, ran almost the entire length of the west touchline to score a try, making the result 3–3, David Chisholm having dropped a goal for Scotland.

As I said, London Scottish against Moseley was the first match I covered. I was on the road, mainly on Saturdays, for twenty-five years, from Melrose to Redruth, from Ipswich to Swansea. I did a few internationals early on, and some county and Services matches, but mostly my assignments were club friendlies, the staple diet then, long before leagues and cups came into being. Even so, there were friendlies and friendlies. Harlequins against Cardiff was a "big" one, seen in terms of the relative strengths of English and Welsh rugby, usually to the detriment of the former. Saracens against Bradford did not have the same resonance, although the play might be as good as anything at Twickenham. Then there were the Oxbridge games against the clubs in the weeks of intensive preparation for the University match. These are scarcely noticed now, more's the pity, but when I started in the Sixties, and all through the Seventies, even into the Eighties, analytical Fleet Street men armed with binoculars would be there in numbers when Oxford met Leicester or Cambridge played Newport.

To another category belonged the touring teams, in all their variety. The first I saw in my professional capacity were the Australians, with their great half backs, Ken Catchpole and Phil Hawthorne, when they beat a combined Neath and Aberavon side at The Gnoll in 1966. (I read last year of Hawthorne's death at the age of fifty-one.) I have also written about, among others, and in no particular order, South Africa, Duendes (Argentina), Atlanta (US), the Proteas (South Africa), Romania, the Netherlands, Buenos Aires University, Fiji, Northern Suburbs (Sydney), Australian Schools, St Albans College (Buenos Aires), Orange Free State University, Italy, Belgium, Japan, Wellington (NZ), Western Samoa, and the New Zealand Under-21s.

An annual preoccupation of mine was the Hospitals Cup, the oldest club rugby competition in the world, going back to 1875. Hospitals teams such as St Mary's used to be a match for many a first-class club, but those days are gone. I reported on the Cup for about twenty years, and it helped me to learn the topography of London, the hospitals' grounds being scattered far and wide, from Mill Hill to Brockley and from Walthamstow to Wimbledon. It was in the nature of the competition that you could never be certain a match would be played where it was due to be. If you did not check before setting out, you could find yourself in the predicament of Rupert Cherry, the *Daily Telegraph* scribe, who went once in good faith to Honor Oak Park in Brockley and found that the match had been transferred at a late hour to Turkey Street in Enfield. So he turned his car round and drove back across London, arriving in time for the final whistle. His report next morning was as comprehensive as ever.

The final was invariably a rowdy affair, rowdier, it seemed, with some hospitals than with others. The medical students and the nurses got up to all sorts of mischief, some harmless, some inventive, some neither. One year a baby elephant hired from Whipsnade was brought to Richmond and exhibited in a van at the Kew end of the pitch. Another year a wall collapsed, injuring spectators. The supporters' horseplay rarely amused Titley, a stickler for conduct, and when he censured them in *The Times* they retaliated by burning him in effigy.

It was before a hospitals match that the referee asked me not to publish his true name because he was supposed to have been at work that afternoon. I suggested J Smith or P Jones but he said the boss might see through those and sack him. Your boss must have remarkable powers of deduction, I thought. The referee then suggested A Wol, spelling it out for me, and I repeated it in puzzlement. "A Wol," he said again, "A Wol – absent without leave." I do not remember who that referee was; but I do remember Chris Ralston, the England forward, playing a prominent part for Richmond in a game at Streatham–Croydon and asking me afterwards not to mention it in my piece, for the same reason. I told him I could hardly avoid mentioning it, and he compromised by asking for it to be kept out of the first paragraph and the headline – which was easy.

It is an ambition of mine to report some sporting event where there are no spectators whatever, not even the traditional man, boy and barking dog. The nearest I have come to this was, in fact, a rugby match, between the London Fire Brigade and the United States Navy, at Hayes in Kent, just before Christmas in 1967. Almost the entire programme that day, including the All Blacks game, had been snowed off, and when I suggested covering this match *The Times*, instantly sensing a significant occasion, agreed.

There were, as far as I could see, which, in the wintry light, was not very far, seven spectators, including the Navy captain, who was injured, their coach, and the author. The Americans arrived thirty-five minutes late, and had to borrow a fireman to make up their number. Both teams consisted of fourteen players, one of whom wore cricket boots. There were no touch judges, and the referee, Peter Kingham, conducted proceedings in an appropriate manner. By mutual consent the match was restricted to twenty minutes each way. The Fire Brigade won 32–0, and I forgot to ask for the names of the scorers. It was coarse rugby in all its hope and glory. And there was a sequel. Late one night the following week, someone from the US Navy, a little the worse for drink, rang the office from his cabin in Mayfair to tell me that I had got one of my facts wrong, although he did not make it clear which. Anyway, that match, with its seven spectators (six, if you care to split hairs and exclude the national press), has remained in my memory while countless others, attended by hysterically cheering multitudes, have gone for ever.

You see, if I remember matches at all, more often than not it is for reasons unconnected with rugby. Another Christmas I was sent to Stradey Park to report Llanelli's game with Bath. I was looking forward to it because I "collect" rugby grounds and I had never seen Stradey. I have still not seen it. The morning papers gave an evening kick-off time and I travelled by the afternoon train. When I arrived the town was deserted and rain-swept. Sheltering in a doorway, I was joined by a policeman and we fell into conversation, as men will when they meet on a desert island. He said he had just been on duty at Stradey and that the match had been poor stuff. Consternation. I telephoned the office with my excuses but, in *The Times* way of things, all they said was, "Fortunes of war, old chap. Happy new year." After that I made a point of checking kick-off times in advance.

The first match I ever saw in England was Northampton against Bath in the mid-Fifties. I was visiting an uncle and aunt at Kettering and my uncle took me to Franklin's Gardens where we stood on the terracing which has long since given place to the Sturtridge pavilion. Dicky Jeeps, Jeff Butterfield and Frank Sykes played for Northampton then and Northampton won 24–0. This was quite soon after the Lions' drawn series with South Africa when Jeeps played test rugby while still uncapped by England. I remember nothing else from that day at Northampton save the luxuriousness, as it seemed to me, of this English ground compared with those I was accustomed to in my north-eastern outpost of Scotland.

The paper sent me, in my early career, to Teignmouth's pretty little ground. Their match was with Brixham, with whom Torquay Athletic and Kingsbridge had discontinued fixtures owing to foul play. I was the fearless investigative reporter but for all I learned there was nothing to investigate. There was, I wrote, not a quiver of controversy and "if there had been it would somehow have seemed as out of place as a Russian battleship on the river

'Dally' Allardice, left, and Johnny Innes after a match for Aberdeen Grammar School FPs in 1948, when they played together for Scotland, Innes as captain. (Allsport/Hulton Deutsch)

Ian McCrae of Scotland clears the ball from a scrum against England at Twickenham in 1967. (Sport & General)

Teign." Officials of both clubs assured me that relations between them had always been good, on and off the field. Brick wall. Full stop. Could any outcome have been more predictable? The match itself, which Brixham won, was "well-mannered but ragged," like a thousand others, "from Twickenham to Tahiti." I have since read "in-depth" pieces that ran to fifteen hundred words and revealed no more than my four hundred.

I also recall a nondescript fixture between the London Welsh and the Harlequins because it was the first – and so far only – match that my wife has seen. She is not sport-minded. She played the obligatory netball at school, tolerates cricket, having been brought up in Surrey at the time of May, Laker, Lock and the Bedsers, and for a couple of seasons revealed an aptitude for bowls. Beyond that, games leave her unmoved.

Old Deer Park that day looked its best: sunlit, deep green, busy with hockey and rugby players, chirpy with spectators, the Kew pagoda exotic above the trees – a fresco of early spring to open out the spirit. There, I thought, is a sight to disabuse anybody of the notion that rugby is all mud and scrums and violence. We went into the pavilion for a cup of tea and then walked across the field to take our seats in the stand. Out trotted the teams and the match began. "Who's that man in yellow?" my wife inquired. "The referee," I replied, proud to be so well informed. "Where do the Harlequins come from?" was her next question. "Twickenham," I said, regretting that, with their picturesque name, they did not come from somewhere less prosaic, such as Wyoming or Timbuktu. A track-suited figure clutching a bucket scuttled on to the pitch. "Is that the doctor?" "No, he's the man with the sponge that heals everything except broken limbs and death." She also wanted to know why the players persisted in kicking the ball over the stand, and why they always passed it backwards when they were supposed to be going forward. She wished there had been a goalkeeper; she felt he would have given a focal point to the game. The variety of scoring confused her. The crowd took umbrage at some of the referee's decisions, and my wife perceived that referees have "a terrible time." Finally, and unprompted, she observed that there was so much whistle that nothing was allowed to happen, thereby showing she has the makings of a true rugby critic.

I suppose the London Welsh, when John Dawes was captain, were the best club side I ever saw. Such was the intoxicating quality of their rugby that a visit to Old Deer Park could be almost an aesthetic as well as a sporting experience. Seven of the Welsh players went with the Lions to New Zealand in 1971, including Dawes as captain: Dawes, the man of whom a section of the national press wrote, when he first played for Wales, that he was only a stopgap until a better centre could be found. Accurate prophecy has never been Fleet Street's forte.

The strange thing about that London Welsh team was their failure to win the national knockout competition, as it was then known, before John Player and Pilkington. They seemed to have everything – until you note that, in the peak years of the Welsh, the competition's winners were Gloucester and Coventry, both forward-based sides. The Welsh were three-quarter-based, as they could afford to be, with Dawes, Gerald Davies, Billy Raybould, J. P. R. Williams, and the rest capable of bewildering any defence. Their forwards, who included Mervyn Davies and John Taylor, were mobile but scarcely all-powerful. On their best days, and there were many of those, still recalled with misty eyes by the Old Deer Park faithful, the whole team ran and handled like backs, quick, daring, improvisatory, making the opposition look leaden.

The Welsh also made a considerable reputation in sevens, but I give the palm to the London Scottish, winners of the Middlesex, Melrose and Hawick sevens, and many more. I first saw them in 1961, during their run of six consecutive finals in the Middlesex tournament. Five of those finals were won and the other, against Loughborough Colleges, should have been. The Scottish evolved and perfected the possession game, sometimes slowing the tempo to a walk, and passing the ball among themselves with controlled casualness, until a gap appeared. Norman Mair said the Scottish did for sevens what the Hungarians did for football, and Mike Williams, who played for Blackheath against the Scottish, wrote that "Their performance was a real revolution, a revelation of what was possible with a little thought, a little practice and a few gifted players." Those players included Robin Marshall, John Brash, Rory Watherston and Cameron Boyle among the forwards, and a backline chosen, over six years, from the likes of Ken Scotland, Iain Laughland, Jim Shackleton, Tremayne Rodd, Ronnie Thomson and Stewart Wilson. Marshall singled out Laughland, the "general" of the side, as outstanding and said – with Rodd, Laughland, Shackleton and Thomson specifically in mind, I imagine – that the balance of the backline would not be matched for a very long time.

Titley in *The Times* vividly described the Scottish style of play: "Unworried, unhurried in their purpose, they dictated the course of affairs to their own convenience, with a cat-and-mouse quality which deliberately lured the opposition into a false sense of assurance before they were torn apart. Deceptively stopping dead, as though in doubt, they would offer the ball as a carrot to a donkey, then snatch it away and bounce off in the opposite direction. Their backing-up in attack and covering in defence enabled them to switch direction at will, so their opponents in turn became perforce cross-eyed and cross-legged."

I used to go to the Middlesex tournament every year, standing on the terraces at the south end, but not now. It has become too popular, too brassy. The sight and sound of fifty thousand people having a good time bring out the misanthrope in me (he is never far below the surface), and the messages boomed over the public address system – about wives accidentally locked in the woodshed, or husbands suddenly called away on business to Alaska – no longer seem funny. Many in the crowd never go near a rugby match at any other time in the season, and go to Twickenham for the sevens only because it is The Done Thing, part of the social calendar, like Wimbledon or Henley, although from time to time they may deign to glance at the pitch in the hope of seeing something thrilling – a streaker, perhaps, or a boy friend scoring a try, or both. These people know nothing about the game and should be barred, don't ask me how, from such occasions; they are depriving genuine enthusiasts of tickets. The Border sports, particularly Melrose, with its family-outing atmosphere, are more enjoyable, perhaps more skilful too.

I have bet on only two sporting events in my life and one was Scotland against Wales at Murrayfield in 1951. Over the lunch-time washing-up I wagered a shilling on Scotland to win. My father said I was daft, and there was logic on his side because the Welsh team had eleven Lions from the New Zealand tour, whereas many of the Scots were young and untried. Scotland won 19–0 and my father would have been delighted to part with a hundred shillings. It was the occasion of Peter Kininmonth's dropped goal. Kininmonth, a back row forward from Richmond, who was leading Scotland, caught a hurried clearance kick by Gerwyn Williams, the Welsh full back, wide out on the Welsh twenty-five, glanced at the posts, and sent the ball between them as if he were a stand-off and did that sort of thing every week. Scotland, their pack usually too light-weight, did not win another game until 1955 – a sequence of seventeen losses, including 44–0 to South Africa – and again Wales were the opposition at Murrayfield; again, too, there was a famous score that turned the match, Arthur Smith's try. He was hemmed in on the touchline when Adam Robson threw him the ball, but he broke away thirty yards, shook off two tackles, punted over another defender's head, tapped on, picked up, and went in at the corner. "Give it to Arthur" used to be the cry at Cambridge, in tribute to a man who was not the fastest of wings but who was one of the cleverest.

Whether as spectator or journalist I have never seen Scotland win at Murrayfield, which is curious. My first visit was in 1953, on leave from the army, when I stood on the terracing on the scoreboard side and watched Wales win 12–0. My last was in 1972, a 14–9 defeat by the All Blacks. I have been luckier at Twickenham. I managed at long range to obtain a ticket in 1959, my first year there, when there was a 3–3 draw; it was 10–8 to England in 1963, the match of Richard Sharp's try, and 3–3 in 1965, as already chronicled; but I was rewarded six years later when Scotland achieved their first success at Twickenham since 1938 with Chris Rea's try and Peter Brown's conversion in the last minute: 16–15. I was also present for Scotland's 22–12 victory in 1983 – and come to think of it there cannot be many people who have seen Scotland win twice at Twickenham. In fact they have won there only four times since the first meeting on the ground in 1911.

What else do I remember about Twickenham? That A. A. Thomson described it as "A noble place to play and a commodious place to watch a game, but a devil of a place to get away from." I would go further and say that the bottleneck before an international is scarcely less congested than the one afterwards; but perhaps, with my dislike of humanity in the mass, I am making out the former to be worse than it is. I also remember that Twickenham is the only ground where I have bought a black-market ticket – for the Ireland match in 1970 – and that the dullest match I ever saw was England against South Africa in 1961. Doug Hopwood scored the Springboks' try in a 5–0 win, and though it was a good one, no try, however well executed, can redeem the other seventy-nine minutes of play if those are sterile. If I went on long enough I might recall a hundred and one other morsels about the Lord's of rugby; but this is not an encyclopaedia.

Sending-offs are commonplace now, the typical game of controlled violence having become less controlled and more violent. An old Surrey player, the late Jack White, who saw Cyril Brownlie, the All Blacks forward, sent off at Twickenham in 1925, once told me that in his day a sending-off was so unusual as to be almost, as he put it, "a hanging offence." I witnessed my first sending-off by chance. I was at Esher for a Saturday morning game and, on my way from the pavilion to the pitch, passed a very tall second-team forward being given his marching orders by a very short referee who scarcely came up to the miscreant's breastbone. It was in that Esher match, incidentally, that I first saw John Horton, playing stand-off for St Helens, and wrote that he showed remarkably mature judgment for a seventeen-year-old. Eleven years later, by then with Bath, Horton was in Bill Beaumont's grand slam-winning England team.

Around the time of the Esher incident, I saw John O'Shea, the Cardiff and Wales prop, dismissed at Coventry, and the changing-room consensus was that he had been unjustly penalized. Where have I heard *that* before? There have also been sendings-off that went unseen by me, even though I was reporting the matches and should therefore have had the benefit of the journalist's all-seeing eye. One was at Bridgwater and Albion, an evening game against Oxford University, and the other during a Hospitals Cup tie at Brockley. Both occurred in a corner of the field, on the press box side, with spectators obscuring the view. I did not learn of the Bridgwater sending-off until too late for the edition, but at Brockley I was lucky enough to overhear someone discussing it in the pavilion immediately afterwards, and was able to inform Rupert Cherry, who had also missed it. A journalist is wise not to be too fussy about the table from which his crumbs fall.

He is also wise not to fret too much about these mistakes; sure as death they are going to happen. Few in my job have not written a report and then received a sarcastic letter from a spectator asking whether they had been at the same match. And not only from spectators. I was once taken to task by an Oxford University Greyhounds centre for writing that his pass had been intercepted by a member of the opposition, the Cambridge LX Club, who scored a try. The centre wrote to me saying it had not been his pass. I remember replying to him, drawing a rather laboured analogy between mistakes made in the confusion of the moment

The 1971 British Lions at Heathrow on their triumphant return from New Zealand. In front, left to right, are the captain, John Dawes, the manager, Doug Smith, and Barry John. (Press Association)

The Scotland team which beat Wales at Murrayfield in 1951. Back row (left to right): D. M. Scott (Langholm), D. M. Rose (Jedforest), N. G. R. Mair (Edinburgh University), H. M. Inglis (Edinburgh Academicals), D. A. Sloan (Edinburgh Academicals), R. C. Taylor (Kelvinside-West), M. J. Dowling (Ireland, referee). Front row: R. L. Wilson (Gala), R. Gordon (Edinburgh Wanderers), R. Gemmill (Glasgow HSFP), A. Cameron (Glasgow HSFP), P. W. Kininmonth (Richmond, captain), W. I. D. Elliot (Edinburgh Academicals), J. C. Dawson (Glasgow Academicals), I. H. M. Thomson (Heriot's FP), I. A. Ross (Hillhead HSFP). (Photograph: Scottish Rugby Union)

on the field and mistakes made in the confusion of the moment off it. I should simply have said, "*Mea culpa*," and shut up.

There are other occupational hazards less obvious to people who merely read newspapers. One is officialdom. I used to dread not being allowed in to the ground because I did not have a press pass, or only had my union card, and it was not unknown for me to funk any possible public argument by paying at the gate. Indeed, I sometimes felt guilty even when I did have a pass and walked in free. It was a vague feeling, hard to explain, possibly rooted in some perverse notion that I was enjoying a privilege I had not earned. Ridiculous, of course, but there you are.

A famous pre-war Welsh international who later became a journalist was once refused admittance to Cardiff Arms Park because he had forgotten his pass and the gateman failed to recognize him. It was like Lester Piggott being refused admittance to Epsom. The famous one was annoyed, partly, no doubt, at this evidence of his fame cutting no ice with a humble official. He had to go home and fetch his pass, like any other hack. With or without a pass, though, I was never refused admittance. "Ah, *The Times*," they murmured at the gate, as if repeating the name of some learned society far removed from rucks and loose ball. "See and give us a good write-up."

I once wrote a piece praising the ladies who make the tea at matches, and it ended thus: "Go along to some rugby grounds, say Rosslyn Park or Saracens, where, before and after the game, you will find the womenfolk serving sandwiches, pies, pasties, sausage rolls, cakes, tarts, scones and biscuits in a cheerful clatter of efficiency. It always looks to me like a labour of love, and it prompts me to ask a topical question: now that women have started playing rugby, will their husbands rush to serve behind the counter? I have to confess that it is not unknown for me to base my written estimate of a match on whether I enjoyed the food there. If it was tasty, I might be kind to a bad match, but if it was stodgy – a rare occurrence – I could be unkind to a good one. Maybe the press, like an army, marches on its stomach."

You can, in fact, see the rugby press, like any professional group, in military terms, with, as ever, a preponderance of foot soldiers – good, reliable reporters – and a small – a very small – number of leading men whose articles are eagerly awaited, not just for the facts, any schoolboy could supply those, but for personal style and forthright opinion. John Reason is indisputably one of the leaders, trenchant, humorous and unafraid, with a vision of the way rugby should be played that he keeps unwaveringly in his mind's eye. Bill McLaren, Hawick's favourite son, has said that in his household there is competition with his wife to see who can lay hands on the *Telegraph* first in order to find out what Reason thinks about the latest big match or talking-point. Characteristically, it was Reason who described Scotland's 1984 grand slam as "the greatest disaster to befall British rugby and the game as a whole since the 1974 British Lions tour of South Africa" because of the (in his view) limited approach of both teams.

I am equally an admirer of New Zealand's Terry McLean, and I believe that anyone combining the best qualities of Reason and McLean would be close to the ideal rugby writer. McLean is less barbed, more romantic than Reason. His *Willie Away* is my favourite rugby tour book, "Willie" being Wilson Whineray, captain of the 1963–64 All Blacks in Britain, and "Willie away" a lineout signal. I re-read it not long ago, and also what Chris Laidlaw wrote about it in his own *Mud In Your Eye*: "Terry McLean's books, with perhaps two exceptions, are masterpieces in their own right, not mere chronicles like all the others. His *Willie Away* is clearly the best of these, a pioneering work in the subtle art of player-to-match writing. By assigning his pen portraiture in a match-by-match sequence, McLean gave the tour book a new cohesion and balance."

Those All Blacks lost their chance of a grand slam when they drew 0–0 with Scotland, a match I saw. The player singled out by McLean was Dennis Young, the All Blacks hooker, who made five heels against the head, including one on his own goal-line when Scotland seemed certain to score. The grand slam, McLean began by saying, lay at the end of the rainbow; and when the match was over he achieved this dying-fall: "Then Murrayfield gathered itself into darkness and the wispy rainbow faded, leaving only the memory of the might-have-beens to be talked of, winter and summer, until even it, too, faded and was gone."

McLean said of Titley that he was "as fine a writer about rugby as could be." Vivian Jenkins, out of his experience as an international player, with its concomitant respect, wrote with clarity and fair-mindedness. Befitting someone brought up in the tradition of the old *Manchester Guardian*, David Frost was cool, elegant and scholarly. Doug Ibbotson does not take the game too seriously, and is none the worse for that; his witty descriptions have been quoted to me. Christopher Wordsworth, a prolific book reviewer when he was not writing about sport, brought to rugby a fertile imagination with a vocabulary to match. Alan Watkins, besides being one of the best writers, has the detachment proper to the best columnists; for enthusiasm, industry and anecdote J. B. G. Thomas could not be excelled; and I have enjoyed Alan Gibson, better known on cricket, but versatile and cultivated enough to turn his pen to various subjects.

And then there was Freddie Edwards, one of the most remarkable men I have known. I doubt if many readers will have come across him, but in spite of – I would prefer to say because of – that fact, he deserves a word here. I first knew him as a schoolmaster at the Aberdeen Grammar. He never taught me regularly and my clearest recollection of that time, during the last war, is of being hauled up in front of him for playing truant, for which he let me off with a caution.

The years passed. I left school, and eventually home, and lost contact with him. When by chance I began to meet him again he had retired from schoolmastering and turned to part-time sports journalism, which suited his restless nature. He had no formal training for the work but he knew and loved sport in a score of its manifestations, and made a small, enjoyable living. He won university Blues at athletics, cricket, football, swimming and water polo, one of them at Cambridge. He played cricket for Aberdeenshire, some reserve games for Aberdeen football club – the Dons – ran the marathon, and sprinted. Once, in his sixties, he turned out for a midweek rugby team when they were short. To the end of his days he was a rugby coach to small boys, and a swimmer.

Freddie wrote mostly about rugby, under the pen-name "Scribe," and cricket, in a sober, factual style in which could be heard echoes of the classroom. When I returned to Aberdeen on holiday he would meet me for coffee in the art gallery, bring me up to date on the local sporting intelligence, and, with gusto and humour, recount his latest journalistic exploits, mistakes and all. The gusto and humour were needed. At the kind of grounds he frequented there were no press boxes, no programmes, often no shelter or telephones – a lack of amenities that would drive some pampered Fleet Street hacks to apoplexy. He had to dig for the simplest information and rely on an old friend, a 1914–18 veteran, to "run" his copy. He used to call himself a Peter Pan, and it was a fair description of one so energetic and interested. His approach to life and sport was boyish, omnivorous, sociable, humble, without cynicism or rancour. Had it been otherwise, I doubt somehow whether he would have lived as long or done as much.

Shortly after his death I visited his widow. She was at a loss to know what to do with his vast accumulation of sporting memorabilia strewn around the loft. We climbed up a ladder to look and she said I could have anything I wanted. The loft was big enough at one end to house a bed, in which, she said, he died one Saturday night. After a day spent reporting, he had climbed up there to sleep, as was his frequent eccentric custom, and when he failed to come down next morning she went and found him. He was eighty years old, and had died among his Wisdens, Playfairs and Rothmans, his Carduses, Robertson-Glasgows, Arlotts and Swantons, his magazines, photographs, notebooks, press cuttings and programmes, going back years and years.

I began this memoir with my father watching Scotland's first grand slam in 1925. He always said he would not see another in his lifetime and he was right. I have now seen two, though not, as they say, in the flesh. In 1984 I was at home in Surrey during the climactic match with France; and in 1990 I was at Melton Mowbray, supposedly reporting on a national indoor bowling final for *The Times*, but in reality crouched before the television set in my hotel room watching England lose at Murrayfield in scenes of extraordinary emotion. How could I have done otherwise after all the provocative word-spinning, public and private, before that 1990 match? My mother was from Sussex, and I love most things English, but when Scotland are playing rugby I am a total Scot.

I have referred to the lineout signal "Willie away." Since it was used by the All Blacks, it was probably more successful than most. But that is only another way of saying it was less unsuccessful; for everybody in the game agrees, tacitly or otherwise, that the lineout is a mess, and everybody, from the International Board to the equally important gentlemen of the Old Pankhurstians pack, has his own remedies for it. The only suggestion I have not seen, perhaps because it is so obvious, is that it should be scrapped altogether.

The lineout creates more problems that it solves. In the unlikely event of nobody being obstructed, lifted or offside, the possession that follows is usually about as much use to the scrum half as a kick in the head, which he may receive anyway as a result of bad tapping or deflecting. As often as not, a maul forms as soon as the lineout breaks up, with no clear advantage to either side. After that may come a set scrum. And so on, one stoppage leading to another.

In place of the lineout, I suggest a football-style throw-in, though not, of course, towards the opposition goal-line. It could be straight across the field or towards your own goal-line, and any distance you like. Think how much simpler the game would become, for players, referees and spectators, and how much more fluid. Unforeseen problems would crop up, no doubt, but they could not possibly be as numerous and frustrating as those of the lineout.

It is when players coalesce, as they do at scrums and lineouts, that the trouble starts and offences multiply. There is, however, a compactness about scrums which makes them superior to lineouts as a means of settling the argument over possession, and gives the ball a better chance of emerging quickly and controllably, with the minimum of interference. There is no compactness about lineouts. They straggle naturally, like ranks of raw guardsmen. Rain or shine, well timed jumping and two-handed catching are rare, and so are successful peels. As for the short lineout, it is as much an admission of failure to solve the riddle of the lineout as it is a tactical ploy. All this means that scrum halves are the most anxious men at lineouts, and look it. Even in international matches there is no guarantee they will be saved by their forwards' skill from a hammering.

If the lineout went, the lineout signal would go too, and that would be a loss to those who see the funny side of the game. In a way the lineout signal is a symptom of what is wrong with the lineout. It is an attempt to shed light on a dark subject, and hardly ever works. You wonder, as you listen to the tense chorus of instruction that precedes the throw-in and watch the confusion that frequently succeeds it, whether these secret codes are worth inventing. One instance is graven on my memory. During a county championship match at Wareham, "Aberdeen" was sung out as a lineout signal. I was gratified to hear the name of my native city being used intelligently instead of to imply a quite fictitious stinginess, but less gratified when the ball flew back over the scrum half's shoulder, and the opposing forwards, rushing through on him, nearly scored.

Nor does it make any difference what kind of signals are used. Numbers are the most popular, but I have also heard girls' names echoing across parks, and authors' names like Charles Dickens, and the names of celebrities like Mickey Mouse. I would have thought it easier to remember names than a string of digits, but who am I to question the significance of 76589314 or 48166735, or even 95246721? The only thing I am sure of, as a humble onlooker, is that they rarely seem to add up in terms of winning the ball.

When I played rugby we did not have lineout signals. We lived in the unscientific, uncoached, unmotivated age, when wing three-quarters, not hookers, threw the ball in. We hatched no plots for the lineouts, we just shambled into position and hoped for the best. The lineout now, whatever the status of the match, is no more satisfactory than it was then, despite all the legislative tinkering. I do not suppose it will be abolished in my lifetime, if ever. It is something to be lived with, like income tax. But contemplating rugby without lineouts is agreeable utopian fun.

The Scotland team which beat Wales at Murrayfield in 1955. Back row (left to right): C. W. Drummond (touch judge), A. R. Smith (Cambridge University), T. Elliot (Gala), W. S. Glen (Edinburgh Wanderers), J. W. Y. Kemp (Glasgow HSFP), R. G. Charters (Hawick), J. T. Docherty (Glasgow HSFP), M. J. Dowling (Ireland, referee). Front row: M. K. Elgie (London Scottish), J. S. Swan (London Scottish), E. J. S. Michie (Aberdeen University), J. T. Greenwood (Dunfermline), A. Cameron (Glasgow HSFP, captain), H. F. McLeod (Hawick), A. Robson (Hawick), W. K. L. Relph (Stewart's College FP), J. A. Nichol (Royal HSFP). (Photograph: Scottish Rugby Union)

Benoit Dauga wins the ball from John Owen at a lineout during the England—France match in 1965. (Sport & General)

My first rugby report for *The Times* was published in March 1965, on Monday the 29th to be exact, and here it is:

London Scottish 14, Moseley 6

London Scottish have a habit of leaving the winning of a match until quite late. They did it again at Richmond Athletic Ground when they beat Moseley by a goal, two tries and a penalty goal to a try and a penalty goal.

They nailed victory to the mast with three tries in ten minutes of the second half. Until then their lead had been confined to an excellent, angled penalty goal, kicked by Wilson in the second minute of the match, and several times they looked like losing it as Moseley mounted eager, crisp attacks whose origins mainly lay in the fluency of Cull and Finlan at half back. Moseley's forwards, too, played rousingly well, their speed at first discomfiting Laughland and Rodd's deputy, McIlvenna, whose service was variable.

But the Scottish defence is breached only by the wiliest rugby, and they bided their time, or seemed to, until that ten-minute period. Then Wilson, who played as Scotland's captain should, turned defence into attack with a long run down the right wing. From the ensuing scrummage a richly flighted pass was bowled to Hodgson who, cutting in suddenly and beautifully, left three defenders stranded and scored under the crossbar. Wilson converted.

At this stage Scottish showed some of their authentic sevens flow and flair, throwing passes in many daring directions, and after Hogarth had twice been held up near the line, Watherston and ten Bos scored a try each.

Moseley retaliated. Ward, their brave full back, kicked a penalty goal, and Abbey who, like Reed and Campion particularly in the pack, pursued the ball as though it were a crock of gold, charged down an attempted clearance by Hodgson and scored at the corner flag.

These were not Moseley's only chances; but Finlan now spoiled his game by kicking fruitlessly and too often, which was not only a pity but also silly, with someone like Hofton, the Warwickshire wing, straining for a run on such a delicious spring afternoon. The result, however, was a just one.

London Scottish: S. Wilson; R. Hogarth, J. Shackleton, G. MacDonald, C. Hodgson; I. Laughland, D. McIlvenna; C. Boyle, I. Walker, F. Payne, F. ten Bos, M. Walsh, J. Brash, G. Orr, R. Watherston.
Moseley: W. Ward; K. Hatter, D. Evans, R. Hazeldine, J. Hofton; J. Finlan, A. Cull; S. Shuck, D. Lane, P. McGowan, R. Campion, P. Robinson, D. Abbey, J. Miller, G. Reed.
   Referee: P. Brook (London).

That was a club friendly, typical of the era, and, fortunately for the beginner that I was, a good one. My last report appeared on December 17, 1990, and entailed rising at five-thirty in the morning; hiring a taxi from Carshalton to Paddington, a distance of some fifteen miles; spending a total of twelve hours in the train to and from Redruth; writing my piece during the return journey in the late afternoon; and falling into bed around midnight.

Cornwall 25, Middlesex 12

The town band had a busy afternoon at Redruth while Cornwall were beating Middlesex in the county championship. Every time Cornwall scored, or did something particularly good, the band struck up a refrain from "Trelawny."

What with that, the ear-splitting local support, the Cornwall team's fire and brimstone, and their own jittery performance, Middlesex were never in the game. But they are still in the championship and, with Cornwall, should qualify from the southern section for the semi-finals.

In perfect conditions Cornwall, who won by two goals, a try and three penalty goals to a goal and two penalties, set out to rattle their opponents and succeeded beyond their expectations. It was ten-man rugby, aimed at inducing mistakes, and it brought Cornwall a 10–3 lead by half-time. Champion kicked two penalties and May, supporting Thomason at a lineout, Cornwall's weakest area, drove through for a try.

Nancekivell, from a scrum thirty metres out, cut inside the cover for another try and Peters touched down the third by the posts when three Middlesex defenders failed to deal with one of his up-and-unders. Wright's try for Middlesex at the end was of only cosmetic value.

Scorers: Cornwall: Tries: May, Nancekivell, Peters. Conversions: Champion (2). Penalties: Champion (3). Middlesex: Try: Wright. Conversion: Fletcher. Penalties: Fletcher (2).

Cornwall: K. Thomas (Plymouth Albion); A. Mead (Plymouth Albion), C. Alcock (Camborne and Royal Navy), G. Champion (Devon and Cornwall Police), T. Bassett (St Ives); W. Peters (St Ives), R. Nancekivell (Northampton); J. May (Redruth), B. Andrew (Camborne), R. Keast (Redruth), G. Williams (Redruth), P. Thomason (Redruth), M. Wesson (Plymouth Albion), A. Bick (Plymouth Albion), J. Atkinson (St Ives).

Middlesex: S. Robinson (Saracens); M. Wedderburn (Harlequins), A. Thompson (Harlequins), C. Smith (Rosslyn Park), J. Doolan (London

New Zealand); M. Fletcher (Saracens), C. Wright (Wasps); A. Roda (Saracens), J. M. McFarland (Saracens); rep: A. Mathewson, Wasps), M. Hobley (Harlequins), M. White (Wasps), N. Provan (London Scottish), J. Fowler (Richmond), M. Rigby (Wasps), C. Sheasby (Harlequins; rep: R. Jenkins, Metropolitan Police).

Referee: E. Morrison (Gloucestershire).

As you may notice, I made no attempt to secure "exclusives" or "quotes." I am not interested in sniffing around changing-rooms or standing at bars. If I want to verify a try-scorer, or find out anything else germane to the match, I go and ask: but that is all. Most "exclusives" are nothing of the sort, having appeared in the entire national press; and "quotes" are statements of the obvious. For better or worse, I have always tried to write the kind of reports that I myself like to read; I want to know what happened on the field, described with some semblance of style and humour. You do not expect a theatre critic to dilate on the actors' domestic lives instead of reviewing the play. Controversy is not my province; in any case, most of it is manufactured.

Two stories, both true, about Bernard Darwin illustrate these points. When he reluctantly went to his first, possibly only, press conference, he walked out in disgust after five minutes, muttering that *Times* readers wanted to know what he thought of Max Faulkner's round, not what Faulkner thought. On the other occasion, Darwin, having written his thousand or so effortless words, was sitting down to dinner when he was told that somebody had just broken the course record. Nowadays this news would make your average golf correspondent rewrite frantically. Not Darwin, not then. Waving the course record aside, he said, "Let the news agencies take care of it," and resumed his study of the menu.

Darwin, by the way, had Welsh blood in his veins, far back, and knew a bit about rugby. He said that Wales's victory over the All Blacks in 1935 was "the greatest contest at any game that I can ever hope to see"; and in *Every Idle Dream*, in an essay entitled "Sherlockiana: The Faith of a Fundamentalist," he speculated on a less exalted but, to some, no less interesting subject:

"I have always wished to know more of Dr Watson's career as a football player, but there is so very little material. All we know (from 'The Sussex Vampire') is that he played for Blackheath when Big Bob Ferguson played three-quarter for Richmond, and once threw Watson over the ropes at the Old Deer Park. Where did Watson play? Not three-quarter or he would have mentioned it. Neither was he fast enough, for though he once declared that he had been 'reckoned fleet of foot', Holmes completely outpaced him in that wild chase after the Hound across Dartmoor. Full back perhaps, a post of which his 'admirable tenacity' might have fitted him, but I doubt it. He was a good, solid, hard-working forward who put his head down and pushed without too much thought. Apparently he had ceased to follow the game when his playing days were over; otherwise when the captain of the Cambridge fifteen asked despairingly what to do in the absence of his crack three-quarter, Godfrey Staunton, Watson would have had some suggestion to make. As it was he showed remarkable modesty in not referring to his feats on the Rectory Field; but what I want to know is what he was doing at Blackheath at all, when he ought to have been playing for Bart's or the United Hospitals. The hospital must have had first call on his services. This lack of loyalty is disturbing. However, we know that after his student days he was either a house surgeon or house physician at Bart's, and it was then presumably when no longer qualified to play for his hospital that Blackheath claimed him."

Those reports of mine, dug from cuttings-books, and landmarks for me, may not interest all readers, but they have the potent value of nostalgia, as the names of old players can be evocative: remember Stewart Wilson, Iain Laughland, Frans ten Bos and John Finlan from thirty years ago? Wilson was a polished full back whose play for the Lions in New Zealand in 1966 was much admired. Laughland, already mentioned as a great seven: footballer, never went on a Lions tour, much to the Lions' loss.

The Dutch-born lock, ten Bos (my father would refer to him as "eleven Bos"), scored a try when Scotland beat Wales in 1962 – their first win at Cardiff since 1927; one commentator said ten Bos charged to the line "like an enraged buffalo." Finlan later formed a very good half back partnership with Jan Webster at Moseley, though they played together only once for England.

"Like an enraged buffalo": was that G. V. Wynne-Jones's simile? I cannot be sure now; perhaps the match was after his time. Wynne-Jones was a radio commentator on rugby, and an eloquent one too, when he had plenty to be eloquent about, with Cliff Morgan, Bleddyn Williams and Lewis Jones in his Welsh teams. Sammy Walker, an Ireland and Lions forward in the Thirties, performed a similar service from Lansdowne Road, his voice soaring into a stratosphere of inaudibility when the Irish pack had the ball at their feet or Jack Kyle and Noel Henderson were breaking through in midfield. Rex Alston, dry, clear and objective, used to share the commentary box with the fruity-toned Wynne-Jones and Walker, and he was an excellent foil for them, just as he was for John Arlott on cricket. Alston, too, had been a player, with Bedford and Rosslyn Park, and knew his stuff. He was a dapper, genial figure in the press box in later years.

Then came television, and with it Bill McLaren – "They'll be celebrating that down at Netherdale tonight." Internationals on the box would not be the same without him: his commentaries are an integral part of the pleasure – conversational, authoritative, forthright yet relaxed, with spontaneous humour. Even the Welsh like him. I enjoy his occasional use of Scottish idiom; once he referred to a confused passage of play as "a mixter-maxter," an expression I had not heard since my youth in the land of oatcakes. Whether it charmed English viewers is beside the point. McLaren has the knack of being completely himself and therefore an authentic personality, as opposed to one of the window-dressed television species. Oddments of sport are all I watch on television and my wife does not watch a thing. We keep a Guide Dogs for the Blind tea-towel draped over the set. Sometimes we talk of dispensing with it, but I always relent, saying I would miss the five nations championship – and Bill McLaren.

Radio commentators are helped by the fact that the listeners cannot see what they see. Television commentators, on the other hand, are almost as exposed as the players. I have my own rule-of-thumb about commentators in general: if they do not embarrass me they must be good, regardless of their sporting knowledge, or lack of it, and regardless of their mistakes, to which they are entitled, like anyone else. Commentators are less important than other easy targets, such as the Government, British Rail and the press, but you would not think so from the volume of insults rained on them. I think their job must be quite difficult and, unlike their envious critics, in the press and out of it, I am sure I could not do it better.

I drew on Bernard Darwin a page or two earlier, for it is one of the minor pleasures of rugby to discover the well-known people outside the game who have been interested in it. Thomas Hughes was not exactly outside the game, but *Tom Brown's Schooldays* is his memorial, not any playing ability of his own. I have covered a match on the Close at Rugby School – the first of the Australian Schools' tour at the end of 1973; they won easily, prompting the *Times* headline "Australian Schools teach rugby to Rugby at

Practice on the playing field of Rugby School *circa* 1923. (Allsport/Hulton Deutsch)

Christian Darrouy dives through Andy Hancock's tackle to score for France at Twickenham in 1965. (Sport & General)

Rugby." Having arrived before lunch, I was wandering among the school buildings in the frosty sunshine when a master, seeing that I was lost, came to my rescue, gave me coffee and sandwiches in his rooms, and arranged for me to meet the Australian manager, Brother Gerald Burns.

Rupert Brooke was a Rugbeian who played for the school, as I believe P. G. Wodehouse did for Dulwich. Samuel Beckett in Paris would not tolerate interruption on a Saturday afternoon when Ireland were playing France on television. John Buchan's novel *Castle Gay* has for its hero Jaikie Galt, a Gorbals lad and wing threequarter, who scores the winning try for Scotland against the Kangaroos; according to A. A. Thomson, the match has nothing to do with the story, but Buchan "simply did not want to let a perfectly good visit to Murrayfield go to waste." Another Scottish writer, Eric Linklater (a former pupil of the Aberdeen Grammar School), describes, in *Magnus Merriman*, Edinburgh on the morning of a Calcutta Cup game:

"In bright blustery March weather, Princes Street is full of tall men from the Borders, brave men from the North, and burly men from the West who have made their names famous in school or university, in county or burgh, for prowess in athletic games. It is not footballers only who come, for on this day all other games do homage to Rugby and admit its headship over them, so that cricketers and tennis players, players of hockey and racquets and fives and golf, boxing men and rowing men and swimmers and cross-country runners, putters of the weight and throwers of the hammer, hurdlers, high and low jumpers, pole vaulters and runners on skis, as well as mountaineers and men who shoot grouse and stalk the red stag and fish for salmon – all these come to see Scotland's team match wit and brawn against wit and brawn of England. To see them walking in clear spring weather is almost as exhilarating as the game itself."

In *England, Their England*, A. G. Macdonell sends Donald Cameron, as part of his education in national rituals, to the University match at Twickenham, where "sixty-five thousand spectators, of whom about thirty thousand appeared to be young men, thirty thousand young women, and five thousand parsons, had packed themselves into their places, the sun had long ago given up the unequal struggle, the mists were massing darkly in the north and east, and a slight drizzle was coming down. The players ran out to the accompaniment of frenzied cheers and counter-cheers, kicked a ball about smartly for a minute or two, sat down for the photographers, stood up for the Prince of Wales, and then set to work."

The London grounds were the first that I got to know at all well as a journalist. I seemed then to be going every other week to Richmond to cover either London Scottish or Richmond – referred to *ad nauseam*, though never by me, as "co-tenants" of the Athletic Ground – but in due course I made the acquaintance of Rosslyn Park at Roehampton, Saracens at Southgate (for many years my local club), Harlequins at Twickenham, London Welsh at Old Deer Park, Blackheath at the Rectory Field (where in the early Sixties I saw Colin Cowdrey score a century), Wasps at Sudbury, London Irish at Sunbury, Metropolitan Police at Imber Court, not to mention Esher at Hersham, the Civil Service at Chiswick, and the United Banks at New Beckenham. The first club I visited outside London was Bedford at Goldington Road, in the heyday of Budge Rogers, and then it was on and on to Coventry at Coundon Road, with its narrow sloping chimney of a press box, Gloucester at Kingsholm, Leicester at Welford Road, Lydney, Bristol, Nuneaton, Blundellsands, Fylde, the Welsh grounds . . .

Some had more character – and characters – than others. You needed cotton-wool in your ears at Coventry and Gloucester, where the support was fearsome in its stridency. Bedford I remember for the perennial Voice in the Crowd, the man who continually counselled referees aloud; he annoyed some but amused me, and I used to consider myself deprived if he was not there, much as a tourist in London might feel if he found Speakers' Corner deserted on Sunday. No infringement was too slight to escape his notice. "Oh, Mister Referee," he would cry, "what about that knock-on by number thirteen? You must have seen it – it was obvious. You can't allow that try." Pause while the referee impassively allowed it. Then: "Mister Referee, that's absurd." In all the years I listened to this man I was never able to pick him out with any certainty, and neither could others in the box.

Jeremy Saywell, though confined to a wheelchair, lived alone in Chiswick and followed Rosslyn Park all around England. He knew the laws of the game as thoroughly as any referee and, seated by the touchline, did not hesitate to point out, so that everybody could hear, what he perceived as the referee's mistakes. He once told me I looked like a priest, for which I forgave him. He also wrote the programme notes, signing himself "Other End, Park." And mention of Rosslyn Park reminds me, in passing, that when we moved house a few years ago, the removal man, name of Ede, I think, told me that he played in Prince Obolensky's last game for Rosslyn Park before his death in a flying accident in 1940. There is a Prince Obolensky Association at Roehampton.

At Blundellsands I saw Middlesex beat Lancashire in a county championship final, two dropped goals to nothing. Tom Brophy at stand-off was expected to be Lancashire's match-winner, but Middlesex reined him in. As always I travelled by train, and when I arrived at Lime Street I took a taxi, and the driver rode me for what seemed like miles along the waterfront to the ground. I have written on England trials at Leicester and Broughton Park, on cup matches at Penryn and Sheffield, on tour games at Exeter and Cardiff. Llanharan is the only ground I have known where the press box was inconveniently positioned at pitch level behind one of the goal-lines; and Grange Road, home of Cambridge University, the only ground where I have heard the players referred to over the public address system as "young gentlemen" and even as "Mister." I have covered schoolboy rugby and women's rugby, the latter a match between Great Britain and France at Richmond. "Many people," I wrote in conclusion, "still find the idea of women playing rugby strange; but Boadicea and Joan of Arc voluntarily took greater risks." (This was quoted in a rugby magazine, as was a remark from another piece of mine: "I distinctly saw Richmond win two lineouts, one in each half.") As for schoolboy rugby, it is always refreshing, and I remember watching – at Richmond, yet again – a future Middlesex and England spin bowler, Phil Edmonds, playing as a back row forward in the same match as Andy Irvine, David Leslie and Peter Warfield; but I did not register anything exceptional about them, though Irvine and Warfield were among the scorers. Irvine was in the centre that day, Warfield at full back.

I have been to most of the principal Welsh grounds, from Newport in the east to Swansea in the west, but only twice to the National Stadium, as distinct from the Arms Park: for Cardiff's game with the 1969 South Africans and for the 1976 Welsh Cup final, won by Llanelli, and given the headline "Saluting Field-Marshal Bennett" because I described David Richards, the Swansea stand-off, as a subaltern in comparison. The South African encounter was blighted by anti-apartheid demonstrations: I remember passing through police cordons to reach the ground, and a fire being started in a corner of the terracing at the city end. Lansdowne Road I have never experienced, although we once spent a holiday in a hotel a couple of pitches' length from it. I have had my voyages of discovery, to Fairlop, Ilford Wanderers, Lower

Sydenham, Upper Clapton, Uxbridge, Kidbrooke, Maidenhead, Sutton and Epsom, North Walsham, Ware. But I will not dwell on my single assignment outside these islands – a match at Poitiers between a France B team and Lancashire, the county champions that year. The coach from Paris was two hours late reaching Poitiers; all of us had to attend an Armistice Day ceremony in the town square the next morning; France B won, with Roger Bourgarel, an Algerian-born Toulouse wing, scoring a try; my report was so disfigured by misprints that I thought the whole expedition a waste of resources; and I was thankful to get home.

It is true, as aforesaid, that I am not one for "sniffing around changing-rooms or standing at bars", but all the same I enjoy the atmosphere of the pavilion, whether or not the camaraderie includes me. I like to go inside before and after the match and move among the crowd, watching the faces and gestures, and listening to the voices, the deep chorus of the game's brotherhood. As entertainment it is often better then the rugby. At lesser matches, hospitals, schools, and so on, where there may be no press facilities, it is with the public leaning over your shoulder that you have to compose your piece and against their noise that you have to try to make yourself heard down the telephone to the copy-takers in the office. Some in my job can dictate "off the cuff" so fluently and well that their stuff is more readable than a considered report; the journalistic maxim that it is dangerous to think too much has a degree of truth. Myself, I prefer to have something written down first. At the more important matches, of course, conditions are much easier. There will be a press room with telephones, refreshments, and folk like team managers and coaches to pass on their wisdom. If you end up being little more than their mouthpiece, and that is increasingly likely, it is nobody's fault but your own. In any case, you will still be read next morning.

When *The Times* achieved its bicentenary in 1985, I had worked for the paper for twenty years, and it occurred to me to mark my own little anniversary be recalling my first day in Printing House Square. What had been happening in sport that distant weekend? For wistful amusement I thought I would turn back to those broad columns and find out. Like every other reader I had forgotten, although of course it had all seemed of earth-shaking importance at the time.

There had been two internationals, England beating France 9–6 at Twickenham and Ireland beating Scotland 16–6 at Murrayfield. "Clarke Key Man Against Uncoordinated French" ran the head-line on the report "From Our Rugby Football Correspondent", who was to be revealed in 1967 as U. A. Titley. Clarke was the scrum half and Weston his stand-off; nowadays they would be referred to as Simon Clarke and Mike Weston, as if we all knew them intimately and never forgot their birthdays, but in those pre-Christian-name times initials were the rule, and even then used sparingly. Titley wrote that "here was vindication for the selectors and triumph for basic Rugby football itself" and that the game was "conducted throughout with chivalrous decorum." Rutherford kicked two penalty goals and the England try came "when Cook steadied himself and passed inwards to Rogers, who made ground before giving Payne a scoring pass in the north-west corner."

Our man at Murrayfield was Rex Bellamy, a brilliant writer on tennis, indeed on any sport that caught his fancy. Concealed behind the byline "From a Staff Reporter," he told us that Ireland were a team reborn. "Under McLoughlin's leadership they no longer rely so exclusively on ruthless resolution and their native flair for the game. They are a well organized, disciplined side, and now gave conclusive proof of it by attaining positive ends with largely negative means." The Irish stand-off was a promising youngster named C. M. H. Gibson who, "with much maturity, quietly harnessed his many gifts for the common good," and dropped a goal that was "a gem of its kind." Scotland's stand-off, Laughland, dropped a goal, too.

"You have names to conjure with there, if nothing else," I wrote. "The actors are different now, and so are many of the critics, but the plots are quintessentially the same, are they not?"

Names to conjure with. I have seen a few, and trust I will see a few more. Here are some, great or good, as I saw them on a particular day or in particular circumstances, starting in the Sixties.

David Watkins, playing for Newport against London Welsh: "He is unusual – a stand-off who is reluctant to part with the ball into touch. Heretically, he prefers it where he can use it, which he did excellently here, one minute inviting his backs to join in the game and get warm, the next inviting the Welsh to try to catch him, and now and again kicking the ball treetop-high, inviting the opposing full back to wait underneath it and not quail."

Gerald Davies, playing for Cardiff against Coventry: "Davies is clearly a great attacking centre in the making. No one who saw him in his Loughborough Colleges days will need reminding of that. He has the speed of most wings, an effortless and exquisite sidestep that deceives his opponents as much as it rouses the crowd, and the instinct to make his thrusts only in the right place at the right time. All he has to do now is prove his brilliance in fiercer fires than club rugby." (Which he did, as a wing.)

Jeremy Janion, playing for Bedford against Bristol: "Janion, who

David Watkins of Wales kicks for touch at Twickenham in 1966. (Sport & General)

Sam Doble in goal-kicking practice at Twickenham in 1972. (Sport & General).

scored a try after a fifty-yard run, played at a slight disadvantage, for the crowd evidently expected him to score almost every time he got the ball. A reputation can be a nuisance. Nevertheless, Janion, though neither a refined mover nor yet an electrifyingly fast one, underlined the value of weight and determination."

Gareth Edwards and *Barry John*, playing for Cardiff against Harlequins: "Edwards and John did enough to show why they are what they are. Edwards's length of pass and strength of break, John's accurate kicking, observant covering, and ability to elude the maximum number of opponents in the minimum of space (called arrogance by the jealous) – there they were, the unmistakeable signatures of two exceptional rugby players."

Sam Doble, playing for Moseley against Bristol: "Doble scored seventeen points – four penalties, a try (by making the extra centre), and a conversion – which he gave the impression of regarding as an average afternoon's work. For him it probably is. Where goal-kicking is concerned, he is better than most for two reasons: he does not often miss and his preparations are not protracted. He comes to kick the ball, not bury it. All he usually buries is the opposing team."

David Duckham, playing for Warwickshire against Gloucestershire: "I doubt whether the ball went to him more than twice. I forget what happened on the first occasion, but on the second he dropped it, to the accompaniment of a cruel cheer. If he had been playing for England those who cheered would have groaned. Still, it is hardly surprising that Duckham should drop the ball. He is not given much of it these days, and when he is, probably drops it from sheer astonishment." (How Duckham's greatness was under-used).

Phil Bennett, playing for Llanelli against Swansea: "He kicked four penalties, including one for a deliberate knock-on, and was unmistakably king of the castle: reading the game, changing the point of attack, kicking for safety or position, and managing his men with the same humorous dexterity. (David) Richards, the

Swansea stand-off, is a good player, but a subaltern compared with the field-marshal who is Bennett."

Dusty Hare, playing for Leicester against Moseley: "Hare is incapable of anonymity in his rugby. No wonder he is so popular with the Leicester crowd, who address him as Dusty, as though each and every one of them were his personal friend. He is never afraid to try something, pops up in unexpected places with faultless punctuality, and rarely fails to reach double figures."

Richard Cardus, playing for Wasps against Richmond: "Richmond could have done with extra players to cope with Cardus alone. He gave them a terrible time, scoring one try, making the running for three others, and exposing their midfield defence. It was the kind of display to have the denizens of the press box reaching for similes about knives slicing through melting butter and bulldozers knocking down tents."

And matches to conjure with? No doubt there were one or two that merited the accolade, but all now lie buried in the results columns of old files. Still, this is my book, and I make no apology for the indulgence of reprinting more brief extracts from my journalism.

Moseley 16, Bristol 11 (December 1966): "Richard Sharp appeared at the Reddings in the role of a candidate for re-election to the England team. He gave a mainly subdued performance in the presence of two selectors. Last week Sharp, in his first senior game for two years, scored two tries and kicked two dropped goals for Bristol against Newport. In the circumstances, that was remarkable, and it would have been doubly so if he had achieved anything comparable here. But he disappointed the optimists, and rarely looked like doing otherwise. The mud was partly responsible. David Watkins might have felt secure on it, but not a man of Sharp's height and sapling build . . . Native ability tells, however, and Sharp showed it from time to time, particularly in the first half. He made one clean break and several half breaks, and he kicked coolly in defence and cunningly in attack. He did little in the second half; but neither did Bristol. Perhaps the two facts are complementary."

Cambridge University 3, Newport 11 (November 1967): "The match at Grange Road had two phases – one visible, the other invisible. During the visible phase – the second half – Newport won. Thick mist came down just before the kick-off, and the entire first half might never have happened, for all that the crowd saw of it. They became possessive about what they did see, so that when the players moved to the other side of the field the deprived spectators uttered plaintive cries imploring them to return."

London Welsh 45, Neath 3 (February 1968): "Other clubs have players as talented, but few have currently advanced as far as the Welsh in instinctive, exhilarating teamwork. Even in a small space their fluency rarely deserts them, so that they can turn the unlikeliest situation to advantage. They do more than play rugby: they revel in it. Against Neath every man looked a virtuoso. Take, for example, the back row of Taylor, Patterson and Gray. Taylor and Gray between them scored twenty points, yet no one should think the less of Patterson because he did not score. All three were astonishing in their pace, power and dexterity."

Royal Navy 13, RAF 6 (March 1970): "Corporal Dennis Brown of the Royal Marines, who plays for Widnes in the Rugby League, scored three tries at Twickenham to help the Royal Navy become Services champions. Brown, an omnivorous wing, comes from the Tiger Bay quarter of Cardiff. He is Welsh on his mother's side and Nigerian on his father's. He is the Navy sprint champion, and in this match he showed why. His tries were vivid examples of speed and opportunism."

Leicester 17, Wasps 3 (February 1971): "If Leicester and Wasps were playing in the Great Unmentionable, a rugby union league competition, both would be in the lower half of the table – the equivalents, perhaps, of Huddersfield Town and Blackpool. They showed why in a disjointed match at Welford Road. Leicester are having a mediocre season, Wasps a worse one. They are on the downward curve of that immutable cycle of good and bad that influences all human affairs, even pastimes. Sooner or later London Welsh themselves, the cornucopia of success, will have a lean period, over the hills and far away though that must seem at present."

Gloucester 16, Coventry 15 (September 1971): "Some of the grandstand critics asserted that Mr Wride was not strict enough. Like the pianist, however, he was doing his best, which was necessarily limited by the fact that he does not have eyes where his ears are and a spare pair in the back of his head as well. In any case, criticizing the referee after a player throws a punch is rather like blaming the doctor for your broken leg."

Gloucestershire 12, Lancashire 17 (March 1973): "Lancashire won a great game of rugby, and the county championship that went with it, at Bristol. The game was not great in skill, as the one between the Barbarians and the All Blacks was. In any case, it was a different sort of game. But it was great in endeavour, suspense and fibre, totally absorbing players and crowd alike. And the better team won, though only just. A downpour before the start left the pitch muddy. It must also have removed any doubts about strategy. Play to the forwards: that would be the first golden rule. Remember the Garryowen kick: that would be the second. Lancashire did both more effectively than Gloucestershire."

Bath 9, Morpeth 13 (March 1975): "Morpeth waded through rain and mud at Bath to reach the semi-final round of the national knockout competition at their first attempt. This was the longest journey Morpeth had ever made. In the ordinary way they play no farther south than Huddersfield. It was a journey that turned out to be strictly necessary. Dismissive things had been said about Morpeth beforehand. But they deserved to win, and Bath agreed . . . So Morpeth have emulated Orrell and become more than a name on the map as far as rugby is concerned. Their joy was unconfined at the end. One of their players even fell on his knees and thumped the earth with his fists, while the red and white scarves tossed and waved in the damp air."

Midlands and North 18, England 10 (December 1975): "The

England trial at Leicester might have been just another club match, as far as quality was concerned. Leicester and Richmond, or Birmingham and Manchester, could have done equally well, probably better, and not only in teamwork either. The Midlands and North beat England, a result that gave much more pleasure to the sceptical crowd than it did to Alec Lewis and his selectors. Their immediate task is to find a team to beat Australia, and they have two more trials in which to do it. Beyond that looms the five nations championship. But as things stand in English rugby, one problem at a time is quite enough."

December 1977: "North Midlands and Gloucestershire, who meet in the county championship final at Moseley, have met once before in the final. That was in 1922, when Gloucestershire won 19–0 at Birmingham. I have been delving into the past to find out about that match. It took place on Thursday, March 9, and ten thousand people watched it in fine weather. Admission prices ranged from one shilling to four shillings. Gloucestershire lunched on the train and after the match the two teams dined at the Grand Hotel . . . Then, as now, Gloucestershire's team contained some famous men: Voyce, Tucker, Corbett, Pickles. All played for England. North Midlands were not so richly provided for, but that was hardly surprising, because their union, comprising mainly second grade clubs, was only formed in 1920 . . . We read of pretty passing, splendid dribbling and close collaring, not to mention scrambling play and faulty handling. We also read that somebody preferred to kick and lost a good chance – and thereby bring ourselves painfully up to date."

Leicester 12, Swansea 19 (October 1981): "It was a match that raised great expectations and satisfied all of them – a rare occurrence. Here was the best team in England pitted against one of the best in Wales. Here, if you must, was an international match in miniature. Here were fine players, an admirable referee, a crowd on tiptoe, and a damp but not disheartening autumn afternoon. And here was Woodward's try. It was scored in injury time at the end of the first half, when Swansea led 6–0 and could have led 26–0, considering the abundance of possession won by their forwards. From a ruck near touch just inside the Leicester half, Kenney stole away on the blind side. The movement spread like a fire. It reached the middle of the field, then turned towards touch again. Finally, it fanned out all the way across to the left, where Woodward, amid deafening enthusiasm, scored in the corner. The ball changed hands twelve times. Cusworth handled it three times. I believe Johnson and Hall were involved somewhere along the line. For a minute or so Swansea were powerless. It was a perfect try of its kind, and Hare gave it the perfect conversion."

England Colts 3, France Youth 16 (March 1982): "It was a pleasant occasion at Portsmouth. The sun shone hazily, the flags fluttered, and the Royal Marines band played and marched. It was a pleasant match, with scarcely one premeditated crash-ball to remind us of routine. The French hinted at why, on their day, they are the best rugby players in the world."

Bath 13, Harlequins 13 (December 1982): "I am glad that I did not have to pay to watch this match because it was the worst I have seen for a long time. There was something appropriate in the fact that both teams scored thirteen points. It was an unlucky occasion to be playing or spectating. If you enjoy listening to the repetitive music of the referee's whistle, you would have had a whole concert of it here. If penalties and stoppages for injury, and yet more penalties, are what thrill you to the marrow, this was your kind of game. If stilted passing, ragged scrummaging, centres doubling back into the forwards, and the odd punch or two are your idea of a Saturday afternoon's entertainment, the Recreation Ground was the place to be for you and your family . . . The programme told us that fifty years ago Bath and Harlequins also drew, 6–6. I was not born then, and have not consulted the files, but I am prepared to swear that it was a masterpiece of a match compared with the one a week before Christmas in 1982."

North 3, London 7 (December 1985): "The North improved their scrummaging but little else at Otley's pastoral ground. They could neither kick their goals nor find a way through, past, over,

under or round the London defence, and the outcome was a
London victory in this divisional championship match. Against
the Midlands the week before the North had the ascendancy for
all of five minutes. They had it for much longer against London –
most of the second half, in fact. But London covered and tackled
well, played with greater purpose, and to that extent were worth
their two scores, one in the first minute, the other in injury time
at the end of the game. . . Not, then, a match to mention in the
same breath as the North's win over the All Blacks on the same
ground. Some of that North team were watching. Heaven knows
what they thought. But London were delighted, full of London
pride, perhaps – that nonsense about the soft city slickers from the
south putting it across the hard northerners."

Great Britain 8, France 14 (April 1986): "Alan Christie, the Great
Britain selector, said that he did not think women's rugby in this
country would start flourishing until the next generation – when
the daughters of the current players take it up. Derek Arnold, the
former All Blacks centre, who helps with the coaching at Wasps,
reckoned that the England men's team could learn from the
women about some of rugby's fundamentals. A collective eager-
ness to run and handle made this an enjoyable match. Fortunately
for spectators, kicking is one of the weaker parts of the women's
game. France scored first, not from a three-quarter movement,
as some of their bold approach work suggested, but from the
pushover try without which no match now seems complete.
Marie-Paule Gracieux, their scrum half, got the touchdown. Later
the French made unladylike comments about one of Mr Leek's
decisions and were penalized an extra ten metres – just like the
men."

Bedford 21, London Scottish 9 (February 1988): "Alwyn Iverson,
of Cumbria, was appointed to referee this match at Goldington
Road but withdrew in good time when he aggravated an old
injury. Somebody forgot to mention it in the right quarter and
consequently they were still scanning the horizon for him just
before the start. But by a curious stroke of chance the referee

Clive Woodward scores for England against Scotland at Twickenham in 1981. Jim Calder is too late to stop him. (Sport & General)

A Scotland player aims for touch in the 1925 grand slam match against England at Murrayfield. (Allsport/Hulton Deutsch)

assessor, Terry Hayward, was there and the whistle was pressed into his hands, although he had not controlled a match for six years. Some of his decisions were unfavourably assessed by one or two players and Orwin, the Bedford captain, was admonished for speaking out of turn. But on any fair assessment of the game Bedford deserved to win, to climb into the upper reaches of the second division of the clubs championship."

The London 9, Royal Free 6 (February 1989): "The London beat the Royal Free by three penalty goals to a dropped goal and a penalty on a wet afternoon at Herne Hill to reach the Hospitals Cup final. . . . The match nearly did not start. The pitch markings were almost non-existent and there were no flag sticks along the touchlines. Eventually the referee decided to do without the markings, but he insisted that corner posts had to be produced. There were other distractions, such as egg and flour battles, and, at half-time, girl streakers. As for the game, the London won mainly because they had a reliable goal-kicker, Maclean, now in his sixth season with them."

A hint of coarse rugby there, I am glad to say, while realising that the Hospitals Cup people take their competition seriously and might resent its being described, however amiably, as coarse. Professionalism may come and amateurism may go but coarse rugby goes on for ever. It is no accident that one of the best books ever written about the game is Michael Green's *The Art of Coarse Rugby*, which will continue to be read long after most of today's productions, ghosted and otherwise, have had their hour and their awards. An inspiring thought. Anybody can play coarse rugby: that is its appeal. It is the rugby of the huge majority. Twickenham is fine in its way but for novelty does not compare with the Old Pankhurstians' ground somewhere in a London suburb – turn right out of the station, cross the road at Tesco's, second left past the Dog and Duck, a hundred yards down a bridle path, through a broken gate beside the clubhouse/shed. Sporting politics, which are even more tedious than the parliamentary sort, cannot taint all this; and neither can professionalism.

In rugby I can forgive anything except dullness. It does not matter to me whether the standard of play is high, low or indifferent, provided a lot happens and I stay awake, and you can take it from me that that can be hard. Another pet aversion of mine is the match with some result such as Old Pankhurstians 31, President's International XV 55. A lot happens there, granted, but it is meaningless, lopsided rugby, with tackling almost non-existent, and where, oh where, is the interest in that? I know these matches may be for a good cause, but they are still a bore. I would ten times rather see a match end 0–0, with a dozen chances missed.

Do you remember the fuss about "boot money" in the Eighties? Every allegation seemed more incriminating than the last. It all feels much longer ago now, with professionalism the norm. Here is something I wrote at the time:

"My rugby-playing career lasted about seven years. My greatest disappointment in that time was not my failure to be chosen for the first fifteen, which I could understand, but the fact that I never found anything in my boots.

How often have I gone into the dressing room before some important match for the third or fourth team, peered inside my boots, and found them devoid even of an Irish sixpence. How often have I tottered from the field at the end of the match, lifted down my jacket from its peg, put my hand in the inner pocket, and come out with no more than an old bus ticket. And a little later when, showered and refreshed, I was enjoying my hard-earned cup of tea, did a sportswear manufacturer disguised as a spectator, a club official or a reporter ever sidle up and make me an offer? Not a bit of it. I endured seven years of such neglect; seven years of mud and blood; seven years of waiting with a cup of tea in my hand; seven wasted years.

The sportswear manufacturers did not know what they were missing. I would have worn anything they wanted me to wear, short of a kilt. Boots would have been only the start (they could have had hollow soles for the cheques). What about the latest fashion in headbands? Of course. Or socks? Pleasure's mine. A jersey with a plunging neckline? Inimitably me, I'm sure. A new brand of jock-strap? I'd try anything once. Price is the only thing I might have haggled over. I am not talking about money: only the dullest dog wants that alone as his reward. If they had wanted to throw in some money as a makeweight I would have been grateful. But the other possibilities would have interested me more.

These sportswear people, it seems to me, lack imagination. They think that money, first and foremost, is what the poor rugby player is hoping to find in his boot. They are wrong. Not all players, not even all prop forwards, are as unimaginative as the manufacturers. A select few, of whom I was one, regard the boot in the same way as they used to regard their Christmas stocking. I know I would have felt hurt and deprived if as a small boy I had opened my stocking and found, instead of toys and books and games and sweets, a bunch of soiled banknotes.

I grew up with this nonconformist attitude almost untarnished. When I was a player money would never have appealed to my romantic instincts. I would prefer to have looked inside my boot and found a charming letter from the manufacturers inviting me to a meeting to discuss a suitable reward. There, over coffee and biscuits (for I am as near teetotal as does not matter), I could have suggested, perhaps, an island of my own in some warm ocean where I could relax during the close season; or a private bowling green or snooker hall, with swimming pool attached, where I could indulge my other pastimes; or, if these were out of the question, the complete works of a dozen of my favourite writers, from Turgenev to Henry Miller, and/or records of a hundred pieces of music I like, from "Calon Lan" (to remind me of Cardiff Arms Park) to Bruckner's seventh symphony.

These are only examples. Depending on mood, I might have asked for something quite different, such as a grand piano or a country bungalow within walking distance of the sea. But they illustrate what I mean about wanting what money can buy rather than the money itself: the ends rather than the means. It would be far more amusing and civilized to do business on those terms than to accept, almost at second hand, that bunch of soiled banknotes, like any old common-or-garden mercenary."

Rugby people are supposed to know as little about football as footballers do about rugby, but as a matter of fact I know a fair amount about football, superficially at any rate. I am rather good at the name game. Ask me Scotland's Wembley Wizards forward line of 1928 and Jackson, Dunn, Gallacher, James and Morton will roll off my tongue like an incantation. Ask me the great Hibernian forward line of the Fifties and Smith, Johnstone, Reilly, Turnbull and Ormond will be a symphony in the ears of those who remember them. And just to prove that I am not insular, did not Matthews, Taylor Mortensen, Mudie and Perry help Blackpool win the FA Cup in 1953, and Jones, White, Smith, Allen and Dyson lead Tottenham Hotspur to the Cup and League double in 1960–61? You cannot ask about modern forward lines because there are none. There are only formations, which are not half so memorable.

I expect you would meet a blank stare if you played this little parlour game in reverse and asked a football follower to reel off back divisions. It would prove that the social differences between the games, though less marked than they used to be, are still an influence. Yet the Oxford University and Scotland three-quarter line in 1925, Smith, Macpherson, Aitken and Wallace, were as fine and famous in rugby as the Wembley Wizards in football, and the Lions combination of 1971, Davies, Gibson, Dawes and Duckham, were as capable of brilliance as the Real Madrid of Puskas and di Stefano. Ian Smith was long-striding and exceptionally fast. In the centre, Phil Macpherson's elusive genius was complemented by the underestimated qualities of George Aitken, who played for the All Blacks four years earlier and has been called "the John Dawes of his day." On the other wing, Johnny Wallace of Australia made up in footballing sense what he lacked in outright speed.

The 1925 grand slam match against England is described in Sandy Thorburn's *The History of Scottish Rugby* in these simple yet sufficient words:

Scotland 14, England 11

"Beautiful weather for the opening of the new ground at Murrayfield brought out a record crowd of at least 70,000 who watched one of the most exciting matches ever played. The lead changed hands thrice and England's great fight to save the game during the last minutes only failed because of some tremendous tackling by the Scots and the utter exhaustion of the attackers.

Luddington had opened the scoring with an early penalty shortly before Macpherson, with a typical dummy and sidestep, broke through and the ball passed via Waddell to Nelson, who, fending off a tackler with a killing hand-off, scored under the posts. Drysdale's conversion put Scotland into the lead but just before half-time England went ahead when Hamilton-Wickes scored after a fine interpassing run with Voyce, and Luddington converted.

Shortly after the restart Corbett had a good run, finishing with a cross-kick which Waddell, on his line, could not hold and Wakefield seized the ball to score. Luddington, when about to take the conversion, was startled to find MacMyn rush out and kick the ball away from the mark – a move accepted by the referee. There followed an excellent try in the right-hand corner by Wallace and a magnificent conversion by Gillies brought the score to 10–11. Wallace had been given an overlap inside the twenty-five and sprinted for the corner, where he dived under Holliday's tackle to touch down just over the line.

Scotland now attacked for the next twenty minutes and several times came near to scoring. Wallace was halted by a forward pass; Scott beat the full back only to be felled by Smallwood cutting across in defence; Aitken dribbled through only to have the ball rebound wide off a goal-post, and Waddell narrowly missed with a drop goal. Then Nelson gave Waddell a clear pass which let him drop a goal from the twenty-five.

With five minutes left England made desperate efforts to score. Smallwood broke away but was floored by Drysdale; Myers was halted on the line by sheer numbers, and finally Corbett broke through only to stumble and fall through sheer exhaustion about a yard short of the line. There remained a final thrill, for Holliday, with practically the last kick of the match, narrowly missed with a very long range drop kick.

Scotland: D. Drysdale (Heriot's FP); I. S. Smith (Oxford University), G. P. S. Macpherson (Oxford University), captain, G. G. Aitken (Oxford University), A. C. Wallace (Oxford University); H. Waddell (Glasgow Academicals), J. B. Nelson (Glasgow Academicals); D. S. Davies (Hawick), J. C. H. Ireland (Glasgow HSFP), R. A. Howie (Kirkcaldy), D. J. MacMyn (London Scottish), J. M. Bannerman (Glasgow HSFP), J. W. Scott (Stewart's FP), A. C. Gillies (Carlisle), J. R. Paterson (Birkenhead Park).

England: T. E. Holliday (Aspatria); R. H. Hamilton-Wickes (Harlequins), L. J. Corbett (Bristol), H. M. Locke (Birkenhead Park), A. M. Smallwood (Leicester); E. Myers (Bradford), E. J. Massey (Leicester); D. C. Cumming (Cambridge University), R. R. F. MacLennan (Old Merchant Taylors), W. G. E. Luddington (Royal Navy), J. S. Tucker (Bristol), A. F. Blakiston (Liverpool), A. T. Voyce (Gloucester), R. Cove-Smith (Old Merchant Taylors), W. W. Wakefield (Harlequins), captain.

Referee: A. E. Freethy (Wales)."

Which is where we began.

To End

There, I have done. I have not told the inside story of rugby. I do not know the inside story of anything. I have not set out on the impertinent task of showing that Rugby football is a good game; rather on the pleasanter duty of thanking all those players and enthusiasts who have given me more than half a century's pure pleasure, from those forwards of the London Irish third fifteen, who in 1912 practically hewed me in pieces like Agag, King of the Amalekites, to those equally exuberant Welsh spectators – all twenty-thousand of them – who virtually tied my ribs in reef knots round a crash barrier at Twickenham in 1954.

A. A. Thomson, *Rugger My Pleasure*
(Sportsmans Book Club, 1957)

But walking back across the flat water meadows, with the cabin lights of the yachts twinkling above the pewter river and Richmond sparkling in tiers through the dusk, I saw the game whole in my mind, dusted it, folded it up, and put it away in the drawer among the lavender sprigs of memory.

Denzil Batchelor, *Days Without Sunset*
(Eyre & Spottiswoode, 1949)

The romance of the game has long gone; professionalism probably means it has gone forever.

Dennis Richards, head of St Aidan's Church of
England High School, Harrogate, in *The Times
Educational Supplement*, October, 1995.